How to SQUID Our Squid Brains*

Como "SQUIDear" Nuestros Squid Cerebros*

*Mejores decisiones, menos arrepentimientos

*better choices, fewer regrets with Quality of Life eXperiments

To you and your loved ones
from the SQUIDminders

including Drs Mel, ZaSm & Zimbardo

version
2022May22

Ready to learn How to SQUID?

We're SQUIDminders. We SQUID our minds and mind our squid. We're here to help you understand how your brain works and how to make better decisions by learning how to SQUID as often as possible.

Stop... ask Questions... Understand... Imagine your choices, then Decide what to do.

Let's get started!

Created by: Dr Zasm and Dr Mel – 🅾 @drmelganus
Illustrated by: Stacey Quigley – 🅾 @quigley_living and
Laboogie – 🅾 @laboogieart
Adaptaciones por Alejandra Levy y el equipo SQUIDminders

Table of Contents

How can we think before we ink?

Whenever you feel like something is wrong, can you

STOP to ask

QUESTIONS to better

UNDERSTAND? Can you

IMAGINE your choices, then

DECIDE on a plan?

You and Your SQUID Brain:
Can You Think Before You Ink?

by Dr Mel & the SQUIDminders

You might be surprised
to learn what we did,
but now we can show you
your very own **squid**!

It's like part of your BRAIN
that is hidden from view,
but it often drives
what you say and you do.

Tú y tu *SQUID* cerebro:
¿Puedes pensar antes de entintar?

por Dr Mel & los SQUIDminders

Te sorprenderá
aprender lo que yo hice,
Ahora te enseño como
tu propio *squid* mentalices.

Es la parte de tu **CEREBRO**
que escondida está.
A menudo lo que dices y
haces el *squid* orquesta.

3

Whenever your **squid** FEELS
like something is wrong,
it's right there to tell you,
it doesn't take long.

It turns different
COLORS
and can make
your heart race.

It can make you get **LOUDER**
or scrunch up your face!

4

Siempre que se SIENTE
que algo anda mal,
Ahí para decírtelo el
squid es el central.

Se transforma
en diferentes
COLORES
y hace que
tu corazón
se acelere.

Puede hacer que tu cara se
ARRUGUE y tu voz se eleve.

5

Your **squid**, it turns out,
will squirt **INK** in distress.
if it feels overwhelmed,
you can make quite a **MESS!**

So what can
you do when your
squid starts
to yelp?

You can
ask some
good questions
if you want to
HELP!

¡Al parecer tu *squid*
en peligro está,
TINTA expulsará y
un grar **LIO** provocará!

Entonces,
¿qué puedes hacer
cuando tu *squid*
se abruma?

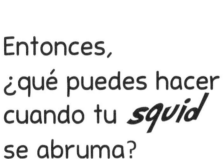

Si quieres AYUDARLE
buenas preguntas
debes hacer,
he aquí algunas:

7

Could you try to distract it before it REACTS?

Could you cover your mouth before it ATTACKS?

Could you take a deep BREATH,

count to TEN, WALK AWAY?

Then ask your **squid** What it most needs to say?

¿Puedes distraerlo antes de que REACCIONE?

¿Puedes cubrir tu boca antes de que ATAQUE?

¿Podrías RESPIRAR hondo,

contar hasta DIEZ?
¿ALEJARTE?

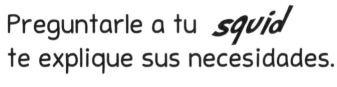

Preguntarle a tu *squid* te explique sus necesidades.

9

Where can you go if you just need to hide?

How can you help your **squid** cool off **INSIDE?**

Could you **STOP** to ask **QUESTIONS** to better **UNDERSTAND?**
Could you **IMAGINE** your choices then **DECIDE** on a plan?

10

¿A dónde te puedes ir si quieres huir?

¿Cómo calmar a tu *squid* INTERNO?

DETENTE un momento para que mejores PREGUNTAS puedas hacer y así a tu *squid* puedas COMPRENDER. IMAGINA tus opciones y DECIDE un plan.

Before you return from where ever you go, make a plan to come back, and try to talk
S L O W...

Things might get messy if your feelings still hurt, but maybe good questions can stop a **squid**
SQUIRT!

Now I have a question that I must ask you! If there's a **squid** in your BRAIN, do I have one, too?

Regresa de donde estás, habla
L E N T O...
evitarás un volcán.

Si tus sentimientos aún
están heridos, las cosas en
caos se pueden volver.
Buenas preguntas evitan que tu
squid ARROJE TINTA
y eche todo a perder.

Te voy a hacer una
pregunta más:
¿Si en tu CEREBRO
un *squid* hay,
crees que en el mío
alguno hay?

13

Why SQUID?

Ever regret something you said impulsively? We have. That's an ink squirt from our Squid minds. We can change the way we make choices. If we can mind our Squid, and SQUID our minds, our lives can get a lot easier.

First, we need to be aware of places in our bodies where we first feel like something is wrong. Before your thinking brain is able to take in what's what, your emotional toad brain is reacting: Fight or Flight or Freeze. Hearts race, our muscles tense-these are your yellow lights. Do we run the red? Or interrupt our autopilot to SQUID?

What is the foundation for our perceived Quality of Life? The stuff going on between our ears, throughout our bodies. Where can we learn about this? Not usually in schools. Kids know more about Tyrannosaurus rex than their own neocortex.

Want to change or start a new habit? If we understood more about neuroscience, we would understand our minds and bodies better. Instead of struggling with academic explanations, SQUID and the Creatures of Habit explain to anyone, any age. Using animal metaphors (like the Creatures of Habit) and memorable step-by-step acronyms (like SQUID) can help us learn and teach how to use the discoveries in neuroscience, psychology and other research.

Our goal is to help people of all ages develop metacognition and mindfulness when we need it most. A huge number of humans, with our squid brains, have contributed to what's here so far, and we need more! Connect with us to learn more about what else we are doing and have for you and your favorite humans?

Find us at QoL-X.org to connect and get the list of what we're working on and the rabbit holes we can invite you into.

Stay curious and open minded. Pay attention to research about our crazy human bodies, and life can get easier!

15

The Creatures of Habit Wheel of Wisdom
Las Criaturas del Habito Rueda de la Sabiiduria

SQUID
Stop
Question   Detente
Understand   Pregunta
Imagine   Comprende
Decide   Imagina
   Decide

ANTS
Activate
Neural   Activa
Trails   Transmisores
   Neurales

HIP
Help   Ayuda
Initiate   Inicia
Programs   Programas

BIRD
Breathe   Respira
Inhale   Inhala
Release   Libera
Direct   Dirige

QOL
Question   Cuestiona
Open   Abre
Listen   Escucha

TOAD
Tense up   Tensar
Open   Abrir
Accept   Aceptar
Defer   Diferir

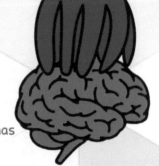

1.6

TOAD(& FROG)
and the CREATURES of habit

TOAD
in BRAILLE

Toad is the **S**
for **S**top in the **SQUID** poem.

EMOTIONS

Name them to Tame them!
You can use the Wheel of
Emotions to help you name
what your feeling.

The Glyphs for Toad

Some doodle
ideas for when
your feelings
are getting
out of hand....
and you just
need a moment.

Tense up body.
Open up body.
Accept?
3**D**'s:
   Defer?
   Deep breathing?
   Distract?

LIMBIC SYSTEM

- Represents all
  the croaking
  in our heads of
  our feelings
  and emotions.

- Toads can be
  poisonous!
  Invasive Cane
  Toads in
  Australia
  are deadly
  to cats who
  eat them.

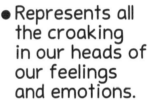

BIRD

and the CREATURES of habit

BIRD in BRAILLE

Bird is the **Q** for **Q**uestion in the **SQUID** poem.

QUESTION

Representing our attentional systems, how we perceive. What we notice through our senses and within our minds.

The Glyphs for Bird

Bird doodles you can try when you need a moment to make sure you ask the right questions.

Breathe
Inhale
Relax
Direct your attention back to your breathing.

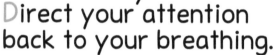

SENSORY CORTEX

- In hyper focused creative problem solving =Crow

- Natural State of mind = Hummingbird

- The sentry

HIPPO
and the CREATURES of habit

HIPPO in BRAILLE

Hippo is the U for Understand in the SQUID poem.

UNDERSTAND

Hippos and other big creatures are like the librarian of our memories. They assign meaning to what we perceive, from the stacks of stored information of experience.

The Glyphs for Hippo

an easy doodle for remembering why we got so ..... upset and to understand why we did in the first place.

Help
Initiate
Positive
Programs
Or else!

HIPPOCAMPUS

- Representing our memories and programs what we learn & forget.

- How we, remember recall recognize.

- Has a love for elephants because they "never forget."

19

Quoll CAT
and the CREATURES of habit

in BRAILLE

Cat is the **I**
for **I**magine in the SQUID poem.

IMAGINE

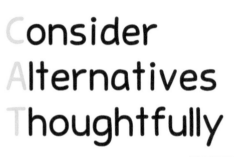

Cat likes to imagine different out comes to the behavior we choose in tough situations.

Which would you choose?

The Glyphs for Cat

Doodles for cat
that a simple, easy,
fun and full of care.
Help you to make
a plan that helps
everyone involved

Consider
Alternatives
Thoughtfully

NEO CORTEX

At its best,
it's a Quoll cat
focused on
maximizing
Quality of Life
for as many
as possible

- At its worst its thoughts and intentions are mean and dark (matched with Toad)

- Example: behaviors of feral and abused cats.

SQUID

and the CREATURES of habit

Sometimes I'm very nervous!!

SQUID in BRAILLE

Squid is the **D** for **D**ecide in the SQUID poem.

DECIDE

Your Squid is the one who decides which plan of action to choose, because you Stopped and took the time to think about the issue you now know there is a better option then just letting your squid ink everywhere.

The Glyph for Squid

Doodle of the Squid is just fun and curvy: how many can you fit on a page?

How to **SQUID!**:
Whenever you feel like something is wrong, Can you **STOP** to ask QUESTIONS before you move on?
Can you ask good questions to better UNDERSTAND? Can you **IMAGINE** your choices, then **DECIDE** on plan?

Nervous System

- Can you THINK before you INK?

- Why are you poking my SQUID?

2.

ANTS
and the CREATURES of habit

ANTS
in BRAILLE

Ants get to be the **!** in
SQUID!

Representing the neurons at the cellular level, communicating through electron chemicals, passed between the key ingredients for every creature of habit and everything we think, feel and do.

The Glyphs for Ant

Doodles for Ant is super easy.
like making a figure eight
but add on an extra loop.
Make a chain of them making a
a path or line,
Now your fully distracted!
Do you even remember
why you were so mad?

Why am I feeling so ANTSY!?

- They are the messagers. They are the ones that relay what the other animals are doing. Like sending a text message, instead of a text a creature of habit sends an ant!

22

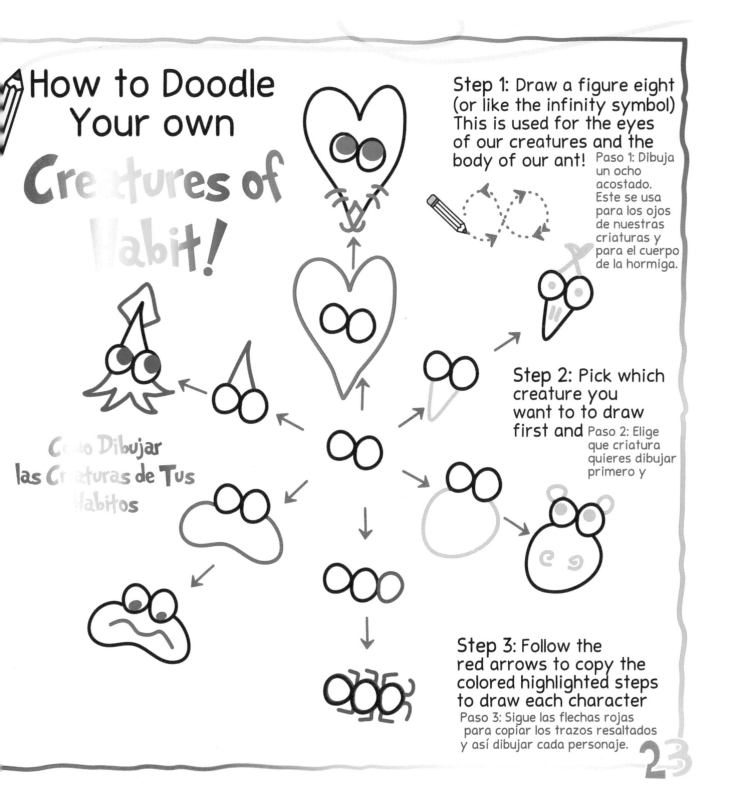

How to Doodle Your own Creatures of Habit!

Step 1: Draw a figure eight (or like the infinity symbol) This is used for the eyes of our creatures and the body of our ant!

Paso 1: Dibuja un ocho acostado. Este se usa para los ojos de nuestras criaturas y para el cuerpo de la hormiga.

Como Dibujar las Creaturas de Tus Habitos

Step 2: Pick which creature you want to to draw first and

Paso 2: Elige que criatura quieres dibujar primero y

Step 3: Follow the red arrows to copy the colored highlighted steps to draw each character

Paso 3: Sigue las flechas rojas para copiar los trazos resaltados y así dibujar cada personaje.

23

There are choirs of creatures inside my mind
Once I knew where to look they weren't hard to find

My Creatures of Habit are my inner voices
They frame my perceptions and drive all my choices

My imaginary friends, some kind and some mean
Live in my squid brain, to you and others, unseen

My squid brain controls what I do and I say
It drives all my choices throughout every day

It pulses with color, swims through life, and can squirt
Especially when I feel scared, angry or hurt

My Bird Brains might notice when something seems wrong.
They fly in to look closely, and ask questions in song.

They are my sensory sentries, paying attention to things,
A sudden sight of red, the loud flap of wings.

My Pachyderm Brains label what my senses perceive,
My Hippo on campus can be quick to retrieve

The memories that my elephant won't let me forget
Especially the times Ive been filled with regret.

My toad brains most often will croak and complain.
They're my emotional systems, my joys and my pain.

24

Whenever they feel like something is wrong,
They flood me with chemistry, it doesn't take long.

My QoL Cats live in my neocortex, behind my forehead.
They've been with me since birth and will stay `til I am dead

They strive to be good, with positive thoughts
They can see my big goals and help connect dots.

Mean Cats live there, too, hiss their thoughts in my ears.
Dark voices, making choices, deeply based on my fears.

Whenever I notice they're getting too loud,
My brain feels foggy, all covered in cloud.

Those clouds turn out to be a constant chemical wash
The choices we make then can turn dreams into squash

My atom ants are the messengers who pass info along
Hormones and neurotransmitters are the notes in our song

When I look in the mirror and imagine all this inside me,
It can seem overwhelming, but it helps me to see

All the noise between my ears, all thew joys, all the tears
My creatures are with me across all of my years.

Which Creatures of Habit are in Your Head?

BEING HUMAN

Have you ever
  Said or done
    Something you regret?
Have you ever
  Hurt someone
    You cared about?
Have you ever
  Been thoughtless?
  Been careless?
  Been unaware?

We have too.
We're human, too.
  Making choices
  Every day.
  Every moment.

We do not control the moment.
We do not control the situation.

But we can do better.
  Better choices.
  Fewer regrets.

The Bubblers

Of "in here" and "out there,"
f us and of others,
Those far and those near.

We listen to some
And ignore the rest.

Open minded or not,
Our lives are a test.

How will we survive?

How will we get through our days?
How can we thrive
When we don't know our ways?

Pray, listen to others,
Listen to your voices within.

We can scream.
We can cry.
We can laugh.
We can grin.

Who are we with others?
Who are we within?

With each new day
We can each try again.

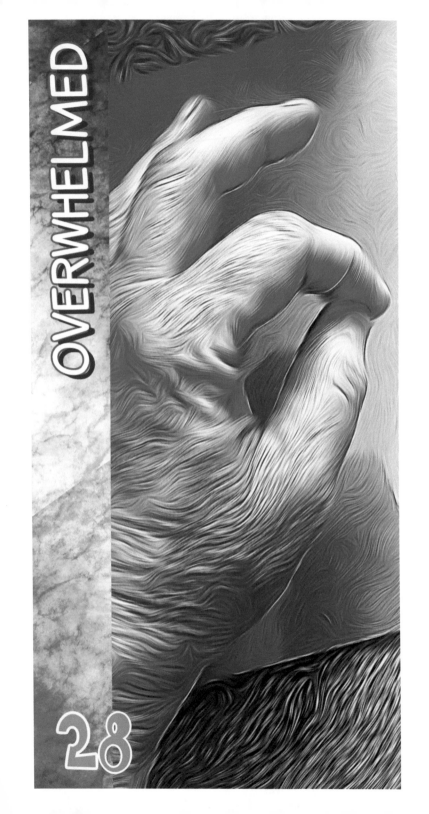

OVERWHELMED

28

When we feel tension in the throat, or tightening in the tummy, tears about to flow, or any "uh-uh," When we begin to feel overwhelmed, About to drown in an emotional flood,

Our responsive system is telling us, "Watch out."

Time to SQUID.

If we pinch our finger

gently, just enough

(we don't pinch others), to distract our emotional brain, long enough for us to breathe

and calm,

get through the moment,

To see what is real,

We can regain balance.

Our Quality of
Life (QoL),
is the sum of
the quality
of our moments.

The quality of our
moments depends
on the quality
of our choices.

Better choices
mean fewer
regrets.

SQUID

Your way to
better choices.

Nuestra calidad
de vida
(QoL-Quality of Life)
es la suma
de la Calidad
de nuestros
momentos.

La calidad
de nuestros
momentos
depende
de la calidad
de nuestras
decisiones.

Mejores
decisiones menos
remordimientos.

SQUIDea

tu vida con
mejores
decisiones.

29

How to S.Q.U.I.D Your mind

Stop- Question- Understand- Imagine- Decide

Step 1: Try to **STOP** when you see squid singles?

The most important step in learning how to "Think Before You Ink!" is being able to notice when your squid is on autopilot or starting to get upset. The faster you notice the signs of trouble, the faster you might be able to do something to help. Your brain has a limit to how much it can focus on, and if you don't help refocus your squid quickly, you might be unable to prevent it from inking. When you do notice your squid is starting to get upset, you want to focus on it quickly to try to help.

Step 2: Try to QUESTION your squid

Your upper brain lights up when you are thinking about things carefully. If you are asking questions, it keeps the lights on in that area, where you have the best chance of thinking before you make choices. Any question might help, but the best questions will be the ones that give your squid a chance to calm down. Could you ask your squid "Do you need a distraction?" Or "Why do I feel like something is wrong?" If you are trying to help someone else, choose questions carefully to help their squid calm down instead of getting more upset.

Step 3: Try to UNDERSTAND the bigger picture

By taking even a moment to look at the bigger picture of what is going on, you can make a better decision about what to do next. Remember to look for more than one perspective about what is going on and why. To improve your understanding, ask yourself more questions. Examples: "Am I overreacting?" "Have I had enough sleep, food, water?" "What's going on for the other people involved?"

Step 4: Try to IMAGINE the possibilities

One of the reasons we ink without thinking is that we aren't imagining what is likely to happen next. When your squid has inked in the past, what usually happens? What do you want to have happen instead? Imagine how other people are likely to respond to different things you could say or do. Use your imagination to come up with some options for what you want to see happen and what you could try to help get there.

Step 5: DECIDE what you want to try next

After taking even a few moments to go through these steps, you can make better choices than if you had never asked your squid any questions. Even if you decide to do what you were going to do on autopilot, you still practiced questioning yourself before you did it. The habit of questioning yourself more frequently gives you many more opportunities to make better decisions. Sometimes you'll still make mistakes, but keep trying! Life gets better!

How to Mind Your Squid

If you can imagine your emotional mind as being *squid-like*, you can watch your squid and notice when it is upset. You can also watch how it reacts to different experiences and feelings, and get better at help How to Mind Your *Squiding* it stay out of trouble and inky messes.

Step 1: Get to know your squid by reflecting on the past

     1. Imagine your lower brain as a squid character you
can see and talk with. Close your eyes. What color is your squid when it's calm? What color is it when it's really upset?

     2. Think about your body and how different emotions show up in your body. If you are starting to get upset, where do you feel it in your body? Does your heart beat faster? Does your face feel hotter? Do you clench your fists or jaw? What do you notice first?

     3. Think about how your squid inks. We are "inking" when we say or do hurtful things to ourselves or others. Do you yell at other people? Do you say mean things to yourself? What types of messes does your squid make that you want to teach it to avoid?

Step 2: Plan for ways you might reduce your squid's inky messes in the future

1. If you can recognize your body's signals that your squid is upset, you can better prepare for responding before your squid inks. What kinds of things annoy you and upset your squid? Can you think creatively about how you could respond in a less messy way next time? What does "Think Before You Ink!" mean to you?

2. If your squid isn't ready for questions, good distractions can be one of the best ways to help calm your squid down. You can "give a gift to your future self" by packing an "Emotional Emergency Kit" into a bag, with different things you love that you could try using to help distract your mind and calm your squid down. Puzzles, games or books that help you focus on something else can be great.

3. In the different places you live and visit, pick somewhere you can go if you get upset. A bathroom might be one of the best escape options and when you are in there, you can check in with your squid, even talking to yourself in the mirror if that helps..

Step 3: Minding your squid during your days and nights

1. Check in with your squid when you wake up. You can care for your squid like a pet, and help it gets what it has to have: food, water, sleep, and love.

2. If you start to notice signs that your squid is getting emotionally upset, pay attention and look for ways to change the direction your squid is going. When your squid does ink, work with it to figure out how to calm down and clean up the mess.

3. Check in with your squid at night before you go to sleep. Help it get a good night's rest so you can start your next day fresh. Squid brains do much better when they've slept.

34

Thought eXperiment:
If good and bad are inseparable,
a yin-yang of the human condition...

eXperimento de Pensamiento:
Si el bien y el mal son inseparables
tal como el yin-yang de la condición humana...

¿Qué es lo qué podemos hacer con esto?
¡Si crees que estás viendo el mal,
entonces puedes SQUIDear!

How can you be an everyday hero?
If you think you see bad,
You can SQUID!

35

Thank You!

So many kind people have helped make these Quality of Life experiments possible - we want to thank you ALL! Thank you for all you do and for being exactly who you are.

And to you who have not yet connected, we enthusiastically invite you to be part of this quality-of-life-changing work! We want to support each of you on your heroic journeys.

Please email squidminders@gmail.com to get links to all the other great stuff we have available to adapt and share wherever you can!

CPSIA information can be obtained
at www.ICGtesting.com
Printed in the USA
LVHW071000100822
725607LV00002B/8